Contents

HAVE FUN PLAYING YOUR

FAVOURITE MUSIC ;)

Clean Bandit - Symphony ft. Zara Larsson

3

Ed Sheeran - Galway Girl

Imagine Dragons - Rise Up

Imagine Dragons - Whatever It Takes

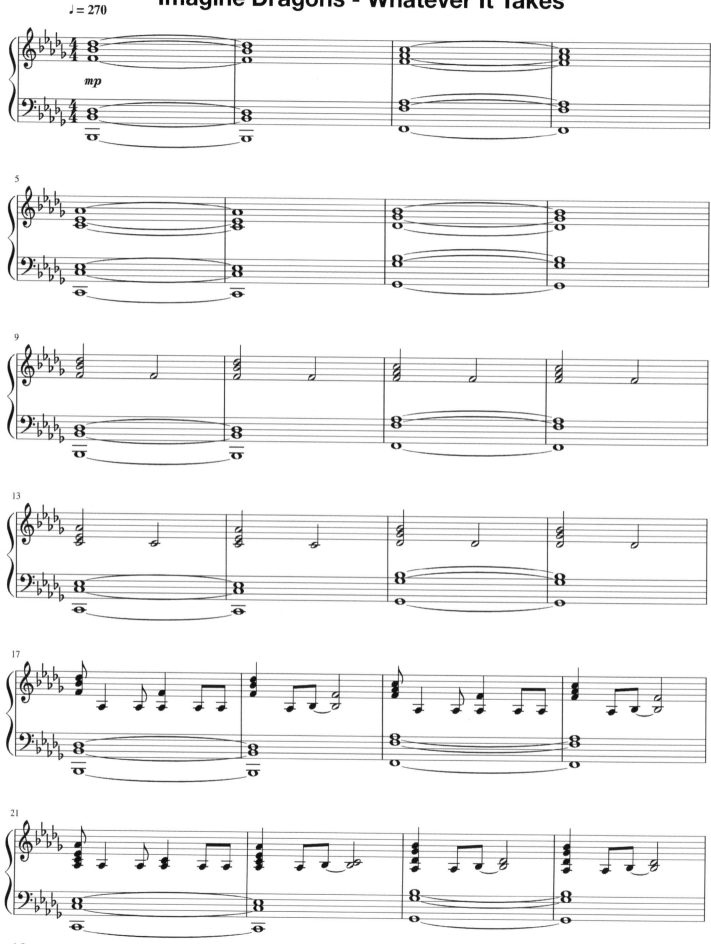

Niall Horan - Too Much to Ask

Taylor Swift - Dancing With Our Hands Tied

Adele - Set Fire To The Rain

Demi Lovato - Cool for the Summer

Demi Lovato - Sorry Not Sorry

would Baby I'm sor – ry I'm not sor-ry Baby I'm sor – ry I'm not sor-ry Feeling inspired

Cause the ta-bles have tur-ned Yeah I'm on fire And I know that it burns

mf Pay back is a bad bitch and Ba - by I'm the bad-dest I'm the bad-dest I'm the bad – dest

Ed Sheeran - Photograph

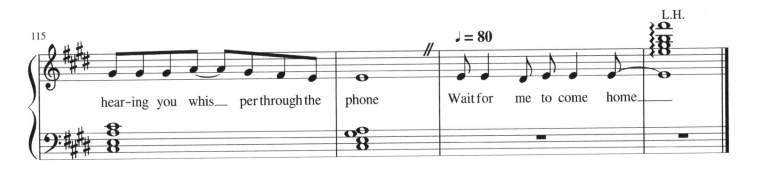

Ellie Goulding - Love me like you do

Beyonce - Crazy in love (50 Shades of Grey)

Coldplay - The Scientist

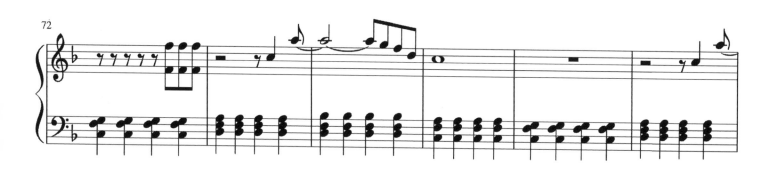

Coldplay - O Fly On

Katy Perry - Firework

Kygo ft. Selena Gomez - It ain't me

La la land - Epilogue

P!nk - Just Give Me A Reason ft. Nate Ruess

Taylor Swift - New Years Day

ZAYN - Dusk Till Dawn ft. Sia

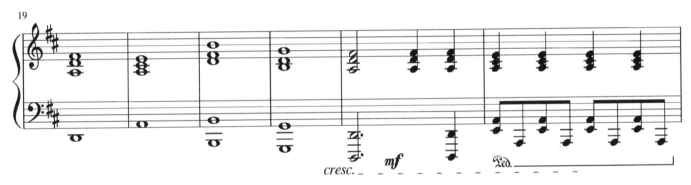

OTHER PIANO BOOKS YOU WILL ENJOY!

Made in the USA
Columbia, SC
18 February 2019